CRAZY TUESDAYS

Courageously choosing fun and free-spirited parenting

Susan Stearns

ISBN: 0615856691
ISBN-13: 9780615856698

Dedication

To Minka and Cooper. I feel so honored that God placed you in my little world for this lifetime. You have shown me more about God's love than you can ever know. May you cling to Jesus through all the adventures of your life. 1437.

Contents

Acknowledgments

To Aaron, thank you for being my best friend.
Thank you for being an amazing husband.
I love you.

To my family both on the Cooper and Stearns sides, thank you for encouraging Aaron and me as we raise your grandkids. Thank you for always giving our kids an endless supply of candy and hugs. Thank you for being there for the frantic calls asking for advice at all times of the night and day.

To all my friends I see face to face and to my friends I just see on Facebook, thank you for liking my status and for commenting on my stories. The connection I feel through sharing stories, comments, and laughs always brightens my day. I hope you realize I only wrote this book because of the constant encouragement from all of you out there.

Last but always first, God. All I have is yours. Thank you for my kids. Thank you for my husband. Thank you for the responsibility of loving them like you love them. May this book bring you honor, and may I always be a light showing your love to everyone who crosses my path.

1
Kids Change Everything

I like to think of myself as a perfectionist—the type of person who excels at everything she does and who notices the details while thinking of the big picture. Yes, I am definitely a perfectionist. I'm just a lazy one. I prefer instant gratification. When I start any type of project, I get so excited that I can't stand waiting for the results for more than a day. So I quickly slap it all together in order to be finished. Be honest—I know I'm not the only one who works out and then quickly runs to the mirror to see the results. Instant gratification!

OK, so maybe I'm not a true perfectionist by definition. However, I do want to be the best at whatever I do. If I am playing a game, I want to win. If I am at the gym, I am constantly pushing myself to run on the treadmill faster and longer than whoever is next to me. I want to always have a clean house. I stress if I have the smallest blemish on my face, and I constantly judge myself harshly if my jeans start fitting tighter than normal. If I make food, I want to be that person everyone calls on for recipes. When I say I am a perfectionist, what I am really doing is just giving my fear of failure a pretty label. Perfectionist. Instead of insecure. Perfectionist. Instead of fearful.

I've always had high standards. When I look back on my life, many of my decisions have been made out of fear.

But then I became a mom.

People always say that being a parent changes you. When I had my daughter, Minka, I changed. My entire outlook on life, my perception of myself and others, my focus, it all changed. Now, naturally you might be thinking this brain bomb happened when Minka was born and the doctor put her sweet six-pound, seven-ounce, little naked body on my chest right after I delivered her. But that's not how it happened. Don't get me wrong, I can still feel the emotions I had when I first saw her face and felt her skin on my skin.

But that was not the moment of my epiphany. When they handed Minka to me, I was thinking more about the last twenty-four-plus traumatizing hours of birthing her and saying I would never again have another child. I believe I was also a bit embarrassed at the moment, regretting that I yelled at the doctor, "Either get her the hell out of me, or take me out back and shoot me like a dog and end this misery. Just save the baby!" Yes, labor changes you.

The moment my world changed was nine days after she was born. I took my husband to Sea-Tac Airport and hugged my soldier and my best friend good-bye as he boarded the plane to go to Iraq and fight for our country. I felt like half my heart had been ripped out as I watched Aaron walk through airport security. My in-laws drove Minka and me home, and once they said good-bye and headed out, I remember shutting the front door behind them and then sitting down on the living-room couch. Minka was asleep in her car seat on the floor.

I sat on that couch and cried for about two hours. They were the hottest tears I ever cried in my life. As I cried those tears, I also felt something I hadn't felt much before—freedom and this magnificent sense of unconditional worth. As I stared at Minka and realized that it was up to me to keep this little person alive, I felt such passion and unconditional love toward her.

I felt freedom because I realized my mom and dad have felt this same way about me the last twenty-three years. And more importantly, I caught a glimpse of what my Heavenly Father feels for me every second of every day. Even when I am insecure and annoying. Freedom. I wanted that little six-pound girl to feel this way as well. I wanted to be an amazing mom.

My focus shifted to living in this new sense of freedom and directing all my energy toward showing her how much Jesus, Aaron, and I love her. I didn't care what people thought of me. I swore to myself in that moment that I didn't care how fast I lost the baby weight or what people thought of me smelling like baby barf and wearing no makeup. I would do my best to live in the moment with my daughter and to raise her in an environment of freedom, not of fear. I felt an excitement, and I felt privileged to have this little person in my life.

Minka is almost four years old now, and we have a one-year-old son, Cooper. This book is made up of our stories. Most of the stories began as status updates on my Facebook page. I hope that in sharing the funny moments, the sad memories, and the challenging days, you can connect. I'm not going to lie; while writing this book, I had moments when I wasn't sure I should be honest, because people I knew were going to read it. Sometimes it took a couple of days to write a story and to be honest and real.

I've also never liked to write. But I've always liked connecting with *real* people right where they are and building connections over *real* issues that we all have in *real* life. As I have talked to my friends who are also parents, and as I have read status updates on FB from friends, I've realized that we tend to all feel the same thing. My stories, my moments, and my emotions...they are other people's stories, other people's moments, and other people's emotions. I want to put a voice to the unconditional love, laughter, and exhaustion that comes with parenting and with life.

So screw fear. My prayer is that you can connect with the stories and be encouraged. Laugh. And most of all—take a deep breath and know that none of us are normal. And yes, other parents feel the same way as you.

2
Green Grass

This last summer I realized how much I love having green grass in my yard. It looks pretty and is fun to play in with the kids. I have never been one to water my lawn at any other time in my life, so I didn't realize how uncomfortable brown grass is to walk on until I suddenly had a green yard. I loved it. From six in the morning until nine at night, on schedule, I moved the sprinkler from place to place, and soon my yard was green and lush.

It was over this same summer that Coop started crawling. I quickly realized that keeping physically active during the day with the two of them led to very good sleep at night for both them and me. So we developed a new tradition in our family. Crazy Tuesdays. On Tuesdays we would go on Pinterest and pick out the messiest craft or activity we could find. Then we would do it outside. It was a brilliant idea. We did all kinds of things, from painting with spaghetti noodles, to mud bubble baths in the pool outside, or just simply using finger paint to paint our bodies as much as we could. It was a blast.

One Tuesday we realized how fun it was to spread a tarp out on the hill in our backyard and cover it in shaving cream and dish soap.

We got it wet and made what we thought was the best slip and slide in the whole world. It was truly epic.

That is, until I realized what shaving cream can do to a lawn.

The next day when I put the tarp away, I saw a twelve-inch rectangle in the exact spot where we slid off the tarp. The shaving cream killed my grass within a matter of hours of coming into contact with it. I was furious. I had worked for months to get this grass pretty so we could play outside. I never missed a day of watering, and I couldn't count the number of times I had to tell M we couldn't play outside because I was watering the grass.

I mean, I was trying to make the grass perfectly green for the kids, right? Or did I want my yard to be a reflection of what a beautiful home we had and what an organized mom I was...

It was then I realized how superficial I was being.

Yes, the green grass was nice to walk in with bare feet and to sit on during picnics. And it did look beautiful and quite put together. But it was clear to me then that if Crazy Tuesdays were to continue as a tradition, it might come at the cost of my lawn. Was I OK with that? Was I OK with not watering on an OCD schedule every day and turning off the sprinkler when M wanted to play outside? I looked outside at my lawn, with its perfect, green lush patches among random dead spots and one big brown rectangle.

Then I remembered making those patches. We did the slip and slide for hours on Tuesday and even had round two when Daddy came home from work. It was the highlight of our week. Those dead patches were symbolic of a really badass fun day. My grass no longer stood out as a well-manicured lawn. But it did stand out to me in a more important way against the backdrop of the neighboring yards that were beautifully manicured. It reminded me of fun memories for my kids and me. I would never put my lawn ahead of making messy memories with my kids again.

3

Justice, Mercy & Humility

"I love you when you sleep, I love you when you are up, I love all your seasons, Mom."

~Minka

Aaron generously offered to take M and Coop to do the grocery shopping, so I could sit in quiet for a bit and work on this book. I grabbed my computer and logged onto FB, which reminded me that I needed to start Minka and Cooper's scrapbook and write down memories for them to have when they are older. Then again... They could just read my Facebook page and get a picture of what we did every few hours while they grew up. My Facebook is like a journal of all the things we have done over the last four years with our two kids. Most of the updates are funny or happy memories, but a few of them are about the more challenging days.

I started by looking at my timeline under 2009 when Minka was born. I hadn't looked at her baby pictures for a long time, and I found myself wondering how time can go by so fast. Have you ever felt that way? I thought that was just something old people said to young people...Uh oh.

I spent the next forty-five minutes crying and laughing as I remembered all the many things we have gone through.

One particular post caught my eye. Minka was three, and Cooper was a few months old. It was a post of the craft we had done that day—a beautiful Instagram-enhanced photo of a canvas with Minka's handprints and footprints, with a verse written on it. I think it got about forty "likes," and everyone was saying what a great idea it was and how they couldn't wait to do it with their own kids. Naturally I was glad the project turned out so well and that people liked the idea. But I also felt slightly pathetic as I thought of what it took to make that cute little canvas.

M has always loved crafts. I love them too. We always try to do at least one craft a day, since our 2013 New Year's resolution was to do one craft a day. I always try to have craft time midmorning to avoid getting too close to nap time, so I don't awaken the Minkers beast. This particular day I had a canvas for her to put her handprints and footprints on. Then I was going to write, "Act justly, love mercy, walk humbly" (Micah 6:8) across her prints. She loves paint, so I figured this craft would be a huge hit, plus it would give me something to hang up in the house. It started out well, but how could it not when your child hears "paint"?

She was a rock star at putting her hands and feet in the paint. And she ever so carefully allowed me to stamp her prints on the canvas. Cooper had amazing timing (pretty sure they were in on this act together), and woke up from his nap right about then.

"Minka, don't move, OK?" I told her. "I'm going to go give Coop his binky, and then I'll wipe your feet off so you can stand up and go wash your hands." She smiled sweetly, and I went to Coop. He went right back to sleep (like I said, he was in on this too), and I quickly grabbed a washcloth and went back to the kitchen, where I had left M.

But there was no M. It looked like a bloody crime scene.

A trail of red footprints led from the canvas all the way into the laundry room. Hand marks were smeared all across the cupboard and walls, making a perfect red-brick road trail to follow.

At that moment I was so angry, I felt like I was in a horror movie and needed to count to ten before I played the madwoman in the scene. I found Minka in the laundry room, hiding behind the door, painting what was left in the paint tube all over her body. Clothes. Hair. Face. I quickly shouted her name. I believe the dialogue went something like this:

Me: "Minka! What the heck! Why did you do this? I told you just wait right there until I come back! We can't do crafts if you aren't going to listen to the rules!"

M (*crying and drooling and clearly crushed*): "I'm soooooorrrrry! I just started painting and couldn't stop! It was so fun!"

I was quite upset about how exhausting it is to do crafts and kept wondering why everything was such a battle. I washed her off, picked up the canvas, and then started cleaning up the paint all over the kitchen and laundry room. As I was washing off the paint, I realized how easily it came off. After all, it was just paint. It took about two minutes and a rag to simply wipe the kid's washable paint off the cupboards and floor.

Minka was nowhere to be seen. She had gotten the vibe and was off playing in the other room. I picked up the canvas to take a picture and put it on FB when I was hit by my own rudeness. Micah 6:8 is my favorite verse. It is the thesis of what I want my life to look like: to act justly, to love mercy, and to walk humbly with my God. I thought of how my awesome craft idea had quickly turned into a bloodbath...a bloodbath of impatience.

I had treated M in a moment of anger with the opposite of justice, mercy, and humility. I strive to show those qualities to strangers, but I couldn't show them to Minka—one of the people I love most in this world.

I hadn't thought about how she is three *and* she had paint on her hands. How could she *not* have wanted to create more while I was out of the room?

I felt horrible. Ah, the moments when good intentions are smashed by a bad reaction and lack of grace. Long story short, I found Minka and talked to her about what I wrote on the canvas and how it was kind of silly that I acted the opposite way. I asked her to forgive me, and we hugged and all was well again. I posted the picture on FB and got my likes and comments. Every time I look at that canvas in the hallway of our house, I am reminded of that day.

My theme verse for my life applied not only to the big things but also to the little things in life as well. Whether I was fighting poverty and changing the world, or just wiping some kid's paint off the floor, I was still called to act justly, to love mercy, and to walk humbly.

4
Girls & Nail Polish

If it were legal and safe to drug our children so they would sleep in, I would totally do it. Since the day she was born, M has always woken up no later than five. I lie awake at night thinking of ways to get her to just sleep in until six. Well-meaning moms have given me tons of advice about how I just have to put her to bed later, take away naps during the day, and wear her out more. Although I know their hearts are in the right place, I despise it when people tell me what amazingly wise act they did to get their child to sleep in until seven or eight. Trust me, we've tried it all, and it has never worked.

When Coop was about four months old, Aaron and I were feeling especially exhausted, so we decided to put a little "morning box" under her bed. We told her when she woke up in the morning, she could get up and open her box and play with the things inside until she was allowed to come out of her room around six. The idea was a hit...for the first morning. The second morning she was bored by the crayons and puzzles. In a moment of desperation, I agreed to her suggestion to put her nail polish in the box. This was a tragic mistake. Had I known what would come about as a result of this choice, I would have banned all nail polish from the house.

Like a lot of girls, M loves her nail polish. She puts a new layer on her toes and fingers just about every day. It's always pink. No other color is ever requested nor accepted.

So Aaron tucked Minka into bed, read her a story, and then reminded her that her morning box was under her bed. He turned off the light and joined me and Coop in the living room for some much-needed relaxation and a movie together. About fifteen minutes into the movie, we hear a shriek coming from M's room. Aaron jumped off the couch and went in to see what the issue was.

I could hear her crying, saying, "Sorry, Daddy! Sorry! It hurts so bad!"

My first thought was that she was faking some injury as a way to get us to come back into her room, but something in her voice sounded like she was actually hurting. That's when I saw Aaron walking slowly down the hall, looking quite pale, and his eyes wide.

"Babe, I think you need to handle this one."

As I made my way down the hall to her room, I was hit by a wall of nail polish, permeating up into my nose and making me feel like I had just inhaled a bottle of the nasty polish. That's when I saw M sitting on her bed. Arms, legs, belly, and feet covered. In pink nail polish. She was crying, and she kept repeating, "Sorry! It hurts!"

I put on my serious face, held my breath, and started to clean up the mess that was all over her body. The crying didn't cease, and she was still complaining of pain. That's when she fessed up.

"Mom, I...ah...painted...ah...my...ahhhh...vajayjay!"

For those of you who don't know that term coined first by Oprah, vajayjay is the word we use for our "privates."

"You did what?"

She repeated what she said. I slowly took a peek. Yep. It was completely and thoroughly painted pink. With pink nail polish.

"I'm so sorry, Mama. I just wanted to be as pretty as a princess."

At that moment I had no idea what to do. Babycenter.com would surely not have an answer for this. *What to Expect the Toddler Years* definitely didn't have a chapter on how to get nail polish off your child's privates. Google? No. So I did what any mom in a panicked situation would do. I called my mom.

She laughed her ass off. Told me definitely not to google it and to give her lots of baths just to soak it off. She emphasized *not* to use nail polish remover.

I'd like to say we removed all nail polish from the house after this traumatizing night, but we didn't. Nail polish is too precious, because of its ability to keep her busy. But we did remove it all from her room and from her morning box.

5

Doctor visits

Raising kids in this day and age can be stressful. Once I had kids, I realized how little I can actually trust other people. My kids are too young to even know how to get on the Internet. So my focus is on things like watching out for stranger danger and not taking candy from strangers; and our concerns focus on public places such as parks and playgrounds. We have weekly conversations with M about this topic, and we have constantly drilled into her head that if anyone even gets close to touching her privates, she is supposed to hit him as hard as she can, scream, and run to her mom or dad. She knows this amazingly well. Whenever we bring up the topic, she proudly repeats it word for word.

"I hit them in the face, I scream, then I come run to you or Dad."

She is always proud that she knows what to do if this situation ever occurs.

When she repeats this scenario back to me, it makes me proud and gives me a little more confidence in her understanding of boundaries and strangers. However, I learned the hard way that sometimes the messages we send to kids are taken to heart more than we can imagine. I learned this on a slightly embarrassing visit to Madigan Army Medical

Center for M's three-year-old well-child visit.

The appointment was going well. M hit all the milestones, and the doctor praised us for her higher-than-average vocabulary and polite manners.

Near the end of the appointment, the doctor (a female) said she would do a quick overall physical exam to see that all was well with M. She checked her arms, her back, her legs, and her balance. She had M lie down on her back, and it all turned to slow motion.

All of a sudden, I realized the doctor's hand was moving to M's upper thigh. I saw M's eyes get wide. She sat up slightly and raised her little hand into the air, bending her elbow at a perfect ninety-degree angle. Her brow furrowed, she drew her arm back cocked and ready, and I realized what was about to happen.

"Stop!" she firmly shouted at the doctor.

I jumped off my seat and snapped out of the shocked state I was in, quickly shouting to the doctor, "Wait!"

Everyone froze, M with her hand in the air, and the doctor with a confused and slightly irritated look on her face. It took a few minutes, but I was able to quietly explain to the doctor that maybe we could skip the rest of the exam for now, and that before the next visit, I would prep M ahead of time about doctors not being "stranger danger" material.

On the car ride home, I praised M for her quick thinking and for being prepared to take action. I explained what happens at the doctor's office and why it's important that we trust them.

I guess we'll find out at her four-year-old well-child appointment if she heard a word I said. Let's hope no one gets the crap beat out of her at that visit.

6
Happy Birthday To Me

Today:

Is my birthday.

I won't see my husband today.

I am sick and running on about four hours of sleep from the past three days.

Both kids are sick and have a scary energy about them.

I left the spoon in the blender when I made Minka her smoothie at five thirty in the morning.

Cooper has thrown up on me eighteen times and counting...

I cried in front of M, and she laughed. :(

I have an exam due in six hours.

And

I have a very. Stinky. Attitude.

To top it off, M keeps saying the phrase I dread the most: "Mom... close your eyes."

When I hear these four little words and see that slightly slanted smile cross her face, I know she is most likely about to do multiple things that she doesn't want me to see. Normally I would enter into a long and educational dialogue with her about why she wants me to close my eyes, and then we would discuss choices and how to make decisions that lead to fun and happy times.

However, by the sixth time she said, "Mom...close your eyes," I decided that I wanted to. It was easier to close my eyes and choose to be unaware of what she was about to do. So I did. Grumpy, sleep-deprived Coop was screaming in my arms, and I just sat down on the couch, held him...and closed my eyes. As soon as I closed them, I heard frantic running down the hallway and toward the back of the house.

I immediately started mentally guessing what my little M would choose to do. Then it occurred to me that she was about to make a choice that would likely result in some "not fun" consequences...and that I was currently making a choice that was "not fun." It was not fun for me. Not fun for Cooper. *Not* fun for Minka. And it wouldn't be fun for Aaron, who would be coming home late that night after a long day at work.

I was choosing to close my eyes.

Let's be honest. Some. Days. Suck. They do. I dislike it when people say, "It's all good" or "There are no bad days." Because, dude, there are. There are bad days. Bad moments. Sometimes bad weeks or months, or even a whole year can be bad. But we still have a choice on those bad days. We can close our eyes, maybe have a bottle of wine at eight in the morning, and feel sorry for ourselves—*or* we can choose to do what is sometimes harder. We can choose to "just keep swimming." Today I choose to keep my eyes open. Tomorrow maybe I will want to close them...or maybe today after nap time, when the kids don't sleep, I will want to close them again. But right now in this moment, I choose to keep them open.

Like M...I have a choice.

By the way, when I opened my eyes, I found M in the laundry room *inside* the dryer eating chocolate candy. But I also saw my handsome boy starring up at me (buggers and all), and I heard M laughing.

Are those two things not the best birthday gifts I have ever been given?

So whatever you are doing today, or tomorrow, think about keeping your eyes open. Sometimes it will probably suck. And be tiring. And hard. *But* you may end up seeing something you weren't expecting.

7

Minka's First Haircut

"Mom, Coop is like my stuff, like my toy.
I'll share him, but if someone tries
to take him away, I will hi-ya them!
And smack them in the face!"

~Minka

Minka was three and a half years old, and she hadn't had a haircut yet. She kept asking, but unfortunately she barely had enough hair to get it cut. Like many babies, I didn't start getting hair on my noggin until I was almost two years old. Minka was the same way. And Cooper...well, I am beginning to wonder if he will ever get hair. So naturally, I didn't have one of those stories about my child chopping off her hair, leaving a funny picture and a trip to Supercuts for damage control.

Until last week...I now have a "the day my daughter cut her hair" story. I also have one of my proudest moments yet as M's mom.

Looking back, I believe this story began when my nephew JD was born with a full head of dark hair. This was a first for anyone in my family tree. We Coopers are always born bald. Naturally, when people would congratulate us on our new little nephew, we were sure to talk up his full head of hair. Apparently this did not go unnoticed by Minka. She has always had a protective and loyal personality, and this was especially true in her passionate love for her little brother.

So one day I was doing dishes, or laundry, or sweeping, or scraping that week's crusted cereal off the kitchen table. I can't remember the exact chore I was doing, but my guess is that I was cleaning. Suddenly I realized no one was saying my name. No one was crying. No one was laughing. No one was watching TV. There was no one. As all of you parents out there know—*not good*!

I quickly scanned the rooms for the kids, and that's when I saw them. In the middle of the playroom sat Coop, smiling as usual and sitting on the floor, staring at me. Next to him sat Minka. She didn't look guilty when she saw me, which I thought was a good sign. Her eyes lit up, she jumped up, and proudly declared, "Look, Mom. I shared my hair with Cooper, so now he has some too! It looks amazing." She ran to me, grabbed my hand, and dragged me to where they had been sitting together.

Sure enough, Cooper did indeed have hair on his head. She had ever so carefully cut a curl off her hair and placed it atop his big bald head. In that moment I could have given her a lecture about cutting things with scissors and blah, blah, blah, blah. But she was so proud of what she had done. How could I do anything but give her a hug and say, "Good job, sweetie." M had seen a need and was willing to give of herself (literally) to help her brother. We had been bragging all week about JD's hair, and Minka simply didn't want her brother to feel bad.

I was a proud mama. Later in the day, we did assign all scissors in the house to a new home—the top drawer in the kitchen. And I talked with her about asking before she does any cutting or slicing of herself from here on out.

Sometimes we talk and lecture and blab until we are red in the face.

We desperately want to raise kids who will contribute to society. Who have manners and watch out for other people. Kids who will make us proud. It was encouraging for me to realize that Minka was listening. Even when I didn't think she was. Our kids do hear us. They get it. If we keep our eyes and our hearts open, we may just recognize their random acts of kindness. Just not in the way we always expect.

8

Pause

"Cooooper...What are you doing in there?
If you want to play, you need to fall out now!"

~Minka, talking to my belly
at eight months pregnant with Cooper

I had just put the kids down for a nap. M kept asking when she and Coop would be able to share a room. I decided the day was going well, with minimal tantrums, so it might be a good time to see how they napped in the same room. The minute I walked out and sat down, it was like a bomb went off over the intercom. The lights turned all red, and despite turning the volume down, I could still hear them laughing in the back bedroom. Occasionally I heard the sound of Cooper crying and M frantically trying to find his binky to plug him up before I came in there. After checking on them and giving M a warning, I realized there was no keeping her out of his bed.

With all the noise, it wasn't the prime environment to sit and write down all the joys of parenting. Or maybe it was the perfect environment. As I listened to them laughing together, I realized it was one of the sweetest sounds I'd ever heard. Yes, I know in another two to four minutes, someone will be crying. But hearing two people whom I love this much laughing together is a pretty big blessing that I wouldn't trade for anything. Not even an hour of peace to write something brilliant.

9

ADVENTURE

"Mom, I just love you. When you get small like me someday, can we be best friends and play at school together?"

~Minka

We live in Washington State, so when the weather keeps us inside, we learn to get creative when it comes to keeping our sanity. They say in our area of Washington, it rains two days a week: one day for three days straight and the other for four. So when the weather does give us a day of even the slightest sun, we try to stay outside all day. Besides boosting our sadly depleted vitamin D, it restores sanity to the kids and to the parents.

We live on an army post, so we put up a little wire fence in the back, giving our Old English bulldog (Dr. Bentley) and the kids room to run without being able to escape. On this particular occasion, it was the first sunny day since we had gotten Dr. Bentley, and since Cooper was able to sit up and play without my assistance. I remember watching Minka play with the dog and run and laugh while Coop sat eating grass and either laughing or crying whenever Minka approached him. It was one of those mental moments that I wish I could bottle up and replay on days full of crying and time-outs, when all I want is seven o'clock to come so I can put the kids to bed.

Later that evening when bedtime finally came, I tucked M in, and she prayed my all-time favorite prayer.

"Jesus, thank you for a fun, fun day," she prayed. "Thank you that Coop is gonna get big and lift me up over the fence so we can go have fun adventures together. Amen!" Suddenly I wondered if those sweet nothings she was whispering in his ear by the fence all day were actually mischievous somethings. I loved what she prayed, because she didn't pray that she would get big and jump over the fence; she prayed that Coop would be big and *lift* her over. And they would run together. And have adventures. That is my prayer too, M. That you and your brother will always lift each other up and run into the adventures together.

10
Santa

"I don't like the little mermaid story, Mom. She didn't need legs like her friend! Jesus made her a mermaid like her mama and daddy, and that's fun! She should put on a shirt too. That's not OK."

~Minka, after reading The Little Mermaid Disney storybook

December 18, 2012, Facebook post:

Noted: M will scream for an hour at bedtime if she thinks Santa is bringing presents. Why? Because according to M, "Nobody comes in our house at night except Grandma and our family. I don't like Santa and his big belly and his bears." I think she meant reindeer. We got her to sleep by saying Santa would knock and Daddy would take the gifts and then Santa would leave.

So Aaron and I have learned that maybe having a tradition of telling our kids that a big, fat, old man is going to sneak into our house while we are sleeping is actually creepy. But because we built up the concept of Santa for months leading up to Christmas, we cannot simply drop him. We will simply have a UPS kind of relationship with the big man from now on.

11
Seven

Seven. The number of times I have gotten short and lost my patience with M for interrupting me today while I try to write. A book. About her and Coop. And how much I love them. Ironic. She couldn't read my laptop screen to know how much I love her. All she knew was that I was doing something with my computer, and every time she asked a question or wanted to sit on my lap, I got annoyed.

Our kids learn what we do and not what we write. Even with the best of intentions as parents, we will still make mistakes. I think what matters is that we keep trying. For every hour I spend writing about how much I love my kids may I spent twice as much time showing them. In my actions and with my words.

12
Courage

For a two-month period in my life, I was a very selfish mom. We had a miscarriage in August 2011, and what followed was a dark eight weeks. It started the day we lost the baby, by buying a bottle of $9.99 wine at the gas station to help me fall asleep. I remember that after several glasses, I stumbled my way to my room, fell onto my bed, and put my right leg over the side to help the room stop spinning. I fell into a deep, dreamless sleep and didn't wake up until eight the next morning. I woke up in the same position I had fallen asleep in, and I woke up with the same ache that had entered my spirit the day before.

My head was pounding, and I was beyond thirsty. I slowly made my way to the kitchen, started the coffeepot, drank some water, took a Tylenol, and then sat on the couch. I felt like shit, and I told myself I would never do that again. But the ache came on again, and I remembered the reason I drank in the first place. The pregnancy was over, and there was nothing I could do about it. I jumped off the couch, ran to the bathroom, and puked.

I spent the rest of the day like any other day. I cleaned, did homework, and played with M. The only difference was that I went to the gas station to fill up the car and found myself buying more wine as well.

I nursed the headache until past noon that day. When four o'clock came around, I was tired and emotionally drained. I needed to relax, and I just needed a good night's rest. *Just one glass of wine to help me chill a little*, I told myself. So while I made dinner, I had one.

I could instantly feel my nerves calm and my mood improve. I was not as sad about the miscarriage, and quite honestly I was a nicer mom and wife. I turned on the usual *SpongeBob SquarePants* cartoon for M before bed and decided to join her on the couch and cuddle before she went to bed. While I sat with her, I had another glass. After the show we brushed her teeth and did story time in her bed before I tucked her in. I could feel the buzz relaxing me already.

Once she was in bed, I decided the dishes could wait. Aaron was working until ten at this time, so I sat down and watched a movie with another full glass. Soon I was tired but didn't ache anymore, so I made my stumbled walk back to the bedroom to pass out again.

Morning greeted me with the same dry mouth and aching head. I guess I drank more than I thought, because the bottle on the counter was almost completely empty. I felt guilty. *Crap. I have a problem. I'll stop. I won't have any wine tonight. It's been days since the miscarriage, and it doesn't make me so sad now...I'll stop.*

At four o'clock that afternoon, stressed and tired, I drank just one glass. Then two. M normally went to bed at seven, but I really needed to relax, so I decided she could go to bed early. She could even have a book in bed so that we didn't have to do story time, and I could get to the couch and my wine sooner. *We can do story time tomorrow night when I am not having such a bad day.*

This continued for almost two months. People didn't ask how I was doing with the miscarriage anymore, and Aaron was still working late every night, so he didn't notice the drinking. The drinking started earlier, sometimes around three o'clock in the afternoon. M's bedtime was officially moved to six thirty, and I graduated to cheap boxed wine as a way to keep myself blind to how much I was really drinking each night.

The headaches each morning became the norm. I learned to have water by the bed and my Tylenol set out and ready for morning.

One morning, while I sat on the couch nursing my headache with coffee and turning cartoons on so M wouldn't nag, I realized something. I watched her sit on the floor watching cartoons and noticed she wasn't even asking me to play with her. It's like she knew I didn't want to. I realized I couldn't remember the last time she had even asked me to read her a story at night. Story time with her used to be my favorite part of our day. We would cuddle up in her bed and just be together. She used to beg for "just one more book."

Now she didn't even ask.

I had created a new normal.

How did this happen? How did I *let* this happen? More importantly, where was I going with this? Where would my life and the life of my daughter and my relationship with my husband be a year from now...or a month from now?

I always drill into M that she has freedom to make choices. Didn't the same truth apply to me? I had choices. And like M, my choices not only affect me but also others as well.

Yes, losing a baby is hard to go through. Yes, drinking started innocently, because I wanted to feel better and sleep. And yes, I was throwing my life away. I was sad that I would miss out on life with a child we would never get to hold. But there was nothing we could do about that. Crap happens. And I was choosing to miss out on memories with my amazing daughter, whom I actually did get to spend this life with. I was denying her the healthy, engaged, sober mom she deserved.

That day I made a choice. I would not let it go on. I would set limits and no longer choose to do what I was doing. I'm not gonna lie; it sucked, and it was really hard some days. No one in my life had a clue I was drinking too much, since Aaron was gone until ten or eleven every night. I maintained good smiles when I was with my family and friends.

I didn't think I would ever share this story with anyone. I have a bachelor's degree in psychology with an emphasis on substance abuse. I knew what I was doing when I started drinking. It was easier to disengage. It was easier to drink than to feel the stress and emotions that were coming with life at that time. Life is hard, and being a parent is exhausting. Sometimes it feels like all I do is mess up as a mom. But I also know I am not alone in these emotions.

I didn't want to share this story because it makes me vulnerable. It lets my friends and family who will read this book see a part of me that I hadn't planned on ever showing. So I debated on this chapter. For a long time.

In the end it all came back to Cooper and Minka. And courage. I want to raise them to be courageous. I don't want them to make choices based on fears and what other people will say about them. Sharing this story with you is scary. But often the things that are the most important in life are scary. So I chose to write it and be courageous. For my kids. And for you, the reader.

We all struggle with different things. Maybe alcohol has never been a problem for you, but perhaps as a parent, some days you feel depressed and put the kids to bed early so you can have time alone with Ben & Jerry's. I don't know your story, but now you know part of mine. And someday when M and Coop read this book, they will know that I struggled—that along with crafts and memories and laughs, our family had hurts and challenges. But they will also know that I chose to be courageous in tackling life head on without holding back. And my prayer is that they will make the same choice. The decision to choose courage.

13
Keeping Fit

I am a nicer mom when I exercise. Prior to kids I played sports and normally had a gym membership wherever I was living. After kids a gym membership was not in the budget, and playing on a local sports team, much less any type of social life, was not on the calendar. So I try to get creative with getting a workout in at least a few days a week. My amazing husband bought me an elliptical about the time I found out I was pregnant with Cooper. The first trimester of the pregnancy, the elliptical remained dusty and untouched. I was too busy puking and being crazy hormonal mama. For the other six months of being prego, I worked out about five days a week. It was great.

Minka didn't seem to agree.

As soon as she saw me tie my sneakers and turn on cartoons for her, it was like the world was ending. She needed a drink, then she was hungry, then she was thirsty again, then the TV was not loud enough, then it was too loud, and so on. She would whine and ask me if I was done yet every two minutes. This all in about thirty minutes. I hated working out and trying to find ways to keep her distracted so she wasn't continually asking me questions. It made me feel even more out of shape, trying to answer all her questions while trying to catch my breath.

But despite all the complaining from her and the stress I felt, it was worth it to get the feeling of those endorphins flowing. That all changed after Cooper was born.

About two months after having Cooper, I decided to start working out again. My goal was thirty minutes a day on the elliptical, at least four days a week. I remember the first time I put Coop to bed, put my sweats and sneakers on, and told M she could watch *SpongeBob* while I worked out and showered.

When I told her this, I immediately had her full attention. *Red flag number one.* She jumped up on the couch, said, "OK," and just started watching cartoons. No complaints. No requests. No whining or tantrum. She almost seemed excited for the time alone. *Red flag number two.* But I loved it. Finally she was growing up and was OK with entertaining herself while I got some much-needed alone time.

For about a week, it was going so well, I decided to work out seven days a week and even take a shower on a few of those days. Life was good. I was clean and getting back into shape, and M was surprisingly helpful in this area. Then...it happened.

Had I known what deciding to clean the laundry-room cupboards would result in, I never would have embarked on this chore. Ever. But I did.

It was a Wednesday morning. I had put off cleaning the laundry room for...well, let's just say it'd been awhile since I had gone through the cupboards. The room is kind of a "if you don't know where to put it, throw it in the laundry room" kind of room. The only drawer that is used for anything specific is the snack drawer I made for Aaron about two months prior. He has a sweet tooth, so being the epic wife that I am, I put all the Halloween, Easter, and Valentine's Day candy in one drawer for him to have candy whenever he wants. For the most part, we don't give Minka candy at home (that is reserved for Grandpa and Grandma), so we told Minka that drawer was Daddy's candy and left it at that.

So there I am, in the laundry room, pulling out the cleaning supplies to organize the drawers, when I see it. Actually, I see *them.* Candy wrappers *galore.* In the back of one drawer, I find about twenty-plus wrappers. Immediately I knew who would be capable of such a crafty act.

My first impulse was to scream her name. But I didn't. I hesitantly opened another drawer and reached my hand to the back. I came up with several handfuls of more candy wrappers. I opened a third drawer, and a fourth. The same thing happened. I stepped out of the room, holding in my words, and saw M playing with her toys. I didn't want to assume it was her. After all, husbands are great at opening something and leaving the wrappers everywhere. Happens everyday.

I knew it was M, but I just couldn't think of how she could possibly find the time to eat all this food without me knowing. We have a crazy-small house, and I am with the kid twenty-four hours a day. Then it hit me. I was not with her twenty-four hours a day. I was with her twenty-three and a half hours a day. Because I work out for thirty minutes *and* take a shower. *Unaccompanied! How could I not see it!* She had been leaving me alone to work out. No complaints. *And* she had not been in the bathroom when I'd been showering. I was so caught up in my new fantasyland that I hadn't realized that's exactly what it was. A fantasy.

She was OK with me working out and showering every morning because she was eating candy the whole time.

I decided I needed to get a confession out of her, so I would have to catch her in the act. Innocent until proven guilty, and boy oh boy, did I know she was guilty.

"Hey, Minka, I'm going to go exercise and shower, OK?"

Her head jerked to me and gave me her full attention immediately—there was that red flag again. "OK, Mom."

"Do you need anything, my *sweetie*?"

"No."

"OK." I walked back to the room, put on my sneakers, and stood there for about two minutes. Just enough time for her to jump off the couch and start her binge session. I quietly walked back into the living room. No M in sight. I saw the laundry room door slightly closed, so I quietly approached and pushed the door open. She had her back to me. I didn't say anything. She held perfectly still.

"Heeeeeeeeeey, Minka, watcha doing?"

She turned to me and smiled. A mouth-closed smile.

"What are you doing, Minka?" She smiled again, keeping her mouth closed and saying nothing. I put my cupped hand under her chin. "Spit it out."

She opened her mouth, and a big yellow chunk of saltwater taffy slid out into my hand.

"Minka, what is this?"

"Candy."

"And what is this?" I showed her wrapper after wrapper and then opened all the drawers to reveal that I had found all her little stashes.

"Garbage from the candy." She looked down, and I knew that she knew she was busted. I asked her if she is supposed to eat from that drawer. She gave me a nice little repeat speech on how it was Daddy's snack drawer and she had to ask to have candy and snacks.

I could have gotten upset and put her on a time-out or given her a lecture that she probably would not even understand or hear. But she had been honest and didn't deny what she had done. She even spit out the candy instead of quickly swallowing it. Instead, I decided this deed deserved a little natural consequence.

"Hey, sweetie, thanks for being honest with me. Don't do that again, OK? If you want candy or a snack, you need to ask me first.

Got it?"

"OK. Sorry!" She was smiling now and seemed relieved at the lack of punishment.

"I have an idea," I told her. "Let's bake some cookies."

"OK!" she shrieked.

We baked our cookies. In an effort to make up for her most recent mistake, I noticed she didn't even to ask to eat any of the batter. The cookies baked while I exercised and she watched cartoons.

A few hours later, I decided it was time for that natural consequence. So I grabbed a couple of cookies and sat down on the couch next to her. I took a bite and commented on how great the cookies we made were.

"Can I have one?" she asked excitedly.

"Oh, sweetie, normally I would say yes. You are always allowed to have a cookie after we bake. But I think you already had your dessert for the day...I can't remember...but didn't you sneak candy today?"

Her eyes looked down, and she quietly mumbled, "Yes."

"I thought so. I guess I will be eating these cookies alone then. Maybe next time you will ask about dessert?"

"OK," she sadly replied. For the next twenty-two-minute *SpongeBob* episode, we sat together on the couch, me slowly eating the cookies and slightly enjoying my creative natural punishment. She, slightly pouting as she watched me take every bite.

I can proudly say we have never had another issue like this. Not because I am such an amazing parent and my kids learn lessons the first time, but because that night I moved all Aaron's candy to a top cupboard she couldn't reach. And yes, about two minutes into my workout the next day, she marched in with her hands on her hips, demanding to know where the snack drawer went.

14
Free-spirited

U rban Dictionary defines free-spirited as "someone who isn't weighed down by the troubles of everyday life, is always themselves regardless of the situation and lives life to the full. Not restricted by other people's opinions."

When my husband and I were choosing a name for our first child, we found the name Minka. The book we found it in said that Minka meant fun and free-spirited. We both immediately knew this had to be our baby's name. Since then I have always told people that her name meant fun and free-spirited. Even when we appeared on *The Ellen Degeneres Show*, I told Ellen that's what Minka meant. However, now that I am writing this book, I can only find other definitions of her name...so far everything says, "strong-willed warrior." Oh well, we still go by that book that apparently shall remain nameless and say Minka means fun and free-spirited.

I love that not only does M's name mean fun and free-spirited, but that she also lives each day in this spirit. Minka loves people. In March of 2012, we started going over to Seattle with a group of people from our church. We would bring lunches, clothes, books, toiletries, and whatever else we had and simply walk the streets of Seattle handing stuff out and talking with people who are homeless.

M still looks forward to that trip that we do once a month to Seattle. I often find her outside in our yard giving pieces of food to any ants she can find. She always says they need food too, since they don't have a home.

She has such a compassionate heart that seeks justice, but sometimes her good intentions embarrass me...and wrongly so, I'm sad to say. On one occasion, as we were walking into a store, a worker holding a sale sign was standing on the sidewalk, waving at cars. Minka grabbed my hand, pointed to the man, and said sternly, "Mom, I need to go tell him something. Seriously, it's so important!"

I didn't know what she had to tell him, but something in the seriousness of her voice told me to walk her over to him. So I did.

She ran up to him and said, "Hey! If you go over to Seattle, I will bring you food and other stuff if you need it, 'cause you don't have a home."

The man was beyond confused by little M rushing up to him and talking in her fast toddler voice. I smiled awkwardly and explained to him that she thought he was homeless. He awkwardly laughed, and we walked away quickly.

I planned on taking M aside before we got into the store so I could explain to her that she can't do that again. But before I got the chance, she proudly said, "Mom! Can we buy some pancakes so when we see him, we can give them to him? He is gonna be so happy when we help him, right, Mom?"

She was so excited to help him. She saw what she thought was someone in need, and therefore it was the natural thing to do for us to offer help to him.

Unlike M, I was embarrassed at her free spirit and courage. But she wasn't. She didn't care what anyone thought. She was doing what she thought was right.

I chose in that moment to spare her a lecture that was beyond her age level of understanding. Instead, I praised her for looking for ways to help people. When we were in the store, I let her pick out extra snacks to bring with us to Seattle that month.

I wish I was more like M in my spirit. I wish I was willing to help people and do the right thing, no matter what people thought. I wish I didn't have such a spirit of fear. So many times I worry about what it looks like to other people. I'm more concerned about being "socially acceptable" than just being a real person who looks out for others. I learned a lot that day. It's a constant struggle, but I am trying to be more intentional in keeping my own adult insecurities to myself as I encourage M to always be free-spirited and courageous.

15
Smile

For a couple of hours, M had been walking around, acting like she had a twitch in her neck. Concerned, I politely asked if she was OK.

"What?" she asked. "Yes. You don't know who I am? I am Pocahontas, and I am flinging my beautiful hair like she does." *Ooooooohhhhh, right. You are beautiful, M!*

As I was saying good night to M, she asked me if I was going to be sitting in the living room when she woke up in the morning.

"Yes, I'll be on the couch with coffee, like every morning, M. Why?"

"Will you be smiling?" she asked inquisitively.

"Yes. I always smile at you when I see you!" I defensively replied.

"I know you always smile, but will you mean it?"

Shame. To think that I would smile at my beautiful daughter and not mean it. Our kids know when we smile and don't mean it. At least toddlers always mean it when they smile. If they don't mean it, they sure as heck won't smile. It's more likely they'll scream or throw something if they are in a bad mood. Toddlers never put on a façade or show us a fake, cheap love. From now on when I look at my daughter, I will smile, and I will mean it.

16
Under pressure

It was July 3 when I learned that I was kind of a jerk sometimes. We were volunteering at the fireworks tent that our church was in charge of. We had been there all day, and M had told me multiple times that she needed to go poop. Nothing makes my blood pressure go up more than to hear, "Mom, I have to go poop" when we are out in public. So I would walk all the way to the bowling alley, since they had graciously agreed to let us use their restrooms for the few days that we were selling fireworks.

Some kids sing when they go number two, some kids take a long time, and other kids are fast poopers. M is like her mama. It's hard to go in any bathroom that isn't ours. When we go anywhere for more than a few days, she inevitably ends up having a tummy ache from lack of bowel movements.

On this particular day, I thought I was in a patient mood. So I was OK with her saying she had to go, making the walk, standing in the stall trying not to touch anything, and reminding her not to touch the seat. I was OK with doing that once. Since I was in a patient mood, I was OK with the second and third attempt that still yielded no poop. But by the fifth time, I was done.

49

"Minka Ana-Del, this is the last time I walk you here to go poop. If you have to go, then *go,* because I am not going to keep standing in here. Just go poop already so we can go back out to the tent and visit with people."

She kept saying she was trying, and I kept losing my patience.

"You have until the count of ten to go poop, and if you don't, then you will just have to wait until we get home because I am not playing this game anymore—"

She interrupted mid-sentence. "Mom! I'm working hard to get my poop out, and every time you say hurry up, you make my poop shoot back up into my butt."

My bad. That's when I realized I was being a jerk. I knew exactly what she was talking about. I knew it was hard to do the nasty in strange places. I was twenty-six, and I still had a hard time doing it. She was three. It was a good reminder that day that little people have the same emotions as big people. By making her feel pressured and nervous when she was doing her best, I wasn't respecting her. I said I was sorry and that I would wait as long as she needed; and if she wanted to, we could take a break and go back out to the tent and try again later.

Plop.

Well, what do you know? I guess she just needed me to lift off some of the pressure. Moms can sometimes be jerks too. Sorry, M.

17
Ellen Degeneres

We were guests on *The Ellen DeGeneres show* in November 2010. She surprised me with flying Aaron home from New York, where he was stationed. She also gave us $10,000 and a new Buick Regal. To say that what she did for our family was a blessing is an understatement. There is no way to express our thankfulness to her. It was the best freaking experience of my life (besides the birth of my children, of course, *wink, wink*).

I was back on the show in November 2012 for her Thanksgiving show, when I had the chance to update her on our family and to thank her again for all she did for us. Because of her gift, we were able to get out of debt and have a reliable car for our family. Not to mention we have some pretty epic memories in Hollywood from the best family vacation we will probably ever have. But there is a continued ripple effect from our experience with Ellen.

Every time I put my kids in our safe reliable car (we named her Ellen), I am reminded how she so generously helped our family with no strings attached. Minka was one when we were on the show. Sometimes I go on YouTube to watch the episode so I can remember how chubby she was when she was that little. She also loves to watch it and talks about how Miss Ellen helped our family. Aaron and I continually talk about what Ellen did for us so that we never forget. So that Minka will grow up knowing how with small acts, you *can* change the world.

The other day it was sunny—a rare occurrence in Washington State—so Minka and I were eating blueberries outside on a blanket, and she was puttering around while I worked on homework. Out of the blue, she said, "Mom, I have a good idea."

In our world, the words "I have a good idea," when coming from M, translate to: *I want to play. Here is what I want to do.* I had to get an essay written that day, so half listening, I said, "OK, M, what?" I hoped she would go play so I could concentrate on homework.

"Mom, let's sit crisscross applesauce and talk about what we are going to do to change the world," she said. "Do you wanna do that?" When I heard that come out of her mouth, I put down my homework and gave her a huge hug. Is that not what it is about? Homework, cleaning, cooking, planning meals for the week, making grocery lists, working out, somehow finding the time to shower at least a few times during the week—those are just activities. Fleeting activities that are obviously important for a healthy, functioning home.

But sitting and talking with M sounded like the best thing in the world. I listened to her tell me her big plans on how she was going to do her part to change the world. How often do we get so caught up in acts of just staying alive during the week in our little bubble that we forget to think of how we can change the world? Thank you, M, for reminding me what Ellen did for us and what we in turn will do for others. And thank you, Ellen, for what you did for our family.

Little acts of generosity. My prayer is not that my kids will grow up and know what my GPA was while going to school full-time and being a mom. Or how clean the house was and how green and perfect the lawn was. My prayer is that Minka will always have the ambition and confidence to want to sit crisscross applesauce on a blanket, eat blueberries, and talk about ways to change the world.

About the Author

S ue Stearns currently lives in Washington State with her husband, Aaron, and their two kids, Minka (four) and Cooper (one). They are proud to be a military family.

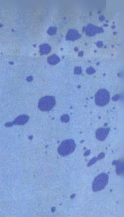

PLEASE EXCUSE THE MESS THE KIDS ARE MAKING MEMORIES

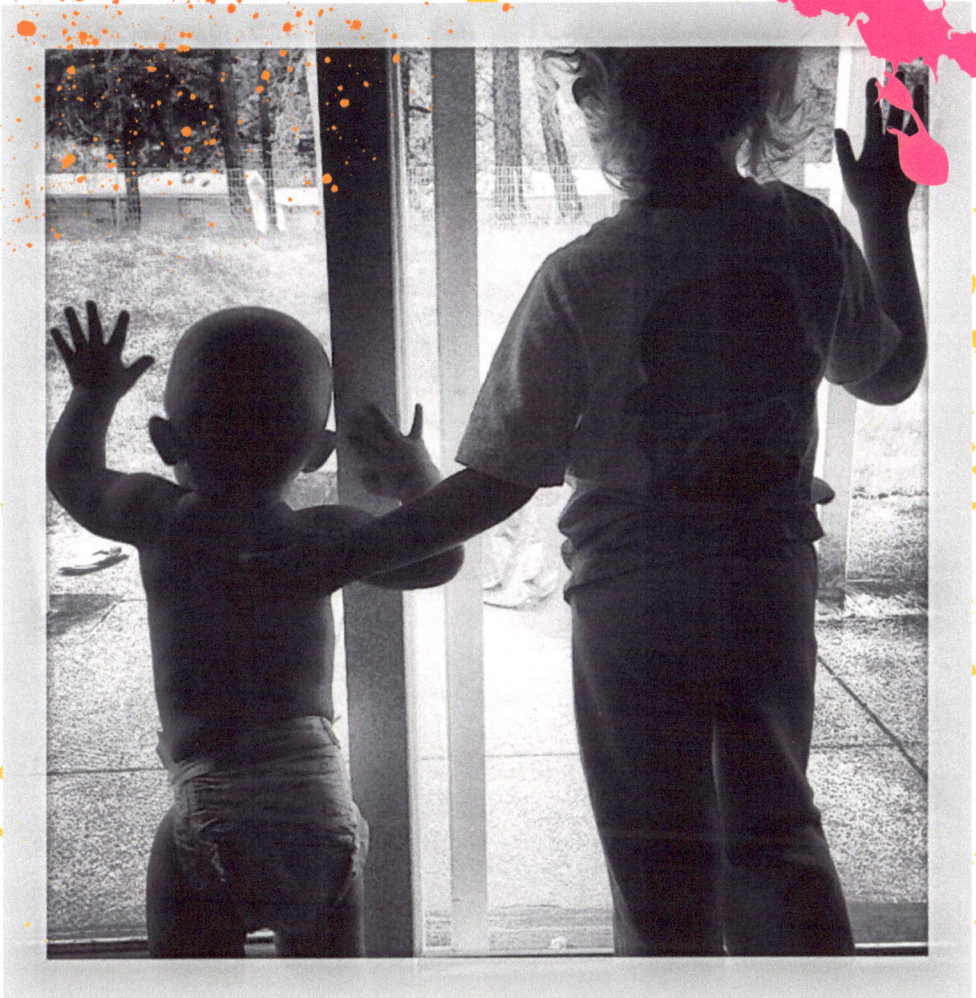

www.ingramcontent.com/pod-product-compliance
Lightning Source LLC
Chambersburg PA
CBHW042126080426
42734CB00001B/16